MY SOUTH KOREA

KOREA

PHOTOGRAPH MEMOIR

DANIEL NARDINI

To order additional copies of this book, contact:
Xlibris
844-714-8691
www.Xlibris.com
Orders@Xlibris.com

ISBN: 978-1-6641-7251-7 (sc)
ISBN: 978-1-6641-7252-4 (e)

Print information available on the last page

Rev. date: 04/28/2021

Contents

Dedication

I wish to dedicate this memoir to my wife Jade Nardini (maiden name Ryu Hwa Soon), and her family back in South Korea. I also want to dedicate this memoir to all of my former students. Without them, I could never have learned so much about South Korea as I did, and for this I will always be grateful to them. Finally, I wish to express my wholehearted thanks and gratitude to the staff at the Sterling Public Library in Sterling, Illinois, for their help. Without their help, this work would not have been possible.

The Magic That is Traditional Korea

I arrived in South Korea as an English teacher for the private English language school ELS Korea and worked there from 1996-1997. I also did correspondence work while living in Seoul for the weekly newspaper *Lawndale News*. After living and working in South Korea, I traveled between the United States and South Korea for the next ten years. Seoul, the capital of South Korea, is a grand city with 10 million plus people. This city has been the capital of Korea since 1394, and has endured foreign invasion, occupation and destruction. With all that Seoul, and indeed Korea, has suffered, it is a miracle that so much from the past is still left. The government and the people have done their best to preserve what cultural heritage has survived. Amid the gleaming concrete and window modern skyscrapers and 21st Century apartment complexes that dot the urban landscape, below and at times hidden away in the thousands of small businesses, corporate offices and modern houses that line the mountains that ring around Seoul, there are the royal palaces, Buddhist temples, and the traditional houses that bespeak of Korea's past.

The beautiful historic sites in Seoul, carefully tucked away amid all of the modern buildings, can be found by both the itinerant traveler as well as long-term foreign resident. This is where traditional Seoul begins. The grand palaces, the Buddhist temples, and other amazing survivors of time are the delight for anyone who has an interest in the cultural and historic aspect of Seoul. Seeing what traditional Seoul has to offer was the highlight for my time in South Korea. Just as equally important were all of the historic sites all through the country. Although Seoul was and remains the capital, the cultural and historic places in so many other parts of South Korea are just as noteworthy of exploration. The former capital of the Shilla Kingdom (57 B.C.E. to 935 A.D.), the City of Gyeongju is a treasure trove of archeological sites as well as temples and ancient artifacts that still exist. Exploring Gyeongju alone could take up to a month of someone's time to see what has endured for over 1,000 years. When the Republic of Korea was founded, most South Koreans tried to get away from their traditional architectural style by building modern concrete and mortar homes and businesses to look more "western." Slowly but surely more South Koreans are returning to the more traditional architectural and cultural style of their ancestors, and with any luck later generations will appreciate what their ancestors from centuries past have left them.

For sure, there is no way that I can even come close to encapsulate the cultural, architectural and historic sites and landscape of this remarkable country. All I can do is provide a very, very tiny fraction of what South Korea has so that those interested in this country can get an idea of the sights, sounds and flavor of what makes Korea **Korean**. This is a personal photographic memoir of some of the most beautiful places I have seen in South Korea. Lastly, Korea would not be what it is without the people who have made the country what it is. Having lived, worked and traveled extensively in South Korea, I came to appreciate the people and all those whom I had worked with, all of the students whom I had taught while working as an English teacher as well as correspondent, and especially my wife and her wonderful family who have given me so much over the years. For me personally, South Korea will always be a magical place that I enjoyed being a part of, and that I hope someday I will to be able to travel there again.

Daniel Nardini
Chadwick, Illinois
2021

A Mountainous Country

A very good friend of mine named Mr. Wang (an ethnic Chinese who was born and raised by Chinese parents in Korea) would go to a Buddhist temple once a week to pray to Buddha and then walk up a mountain for exercise. I joined him walking up the mountain. While he walked slowly, he managed to get up the mountain without too much trouble. The monks had constructed earthen walk steps up to the crest of the mountain. Even with these, I got winded pretty fast because I came from an area where the geography is level. When we got to the top, Mr. Wang would look towards the other areas of Seoul and the other mountains in the distance.

Seventy percent of South Korea is mountain, so mountains play a major role in Korean culture and history. When Korea was invaded, Koreans fled to the mountains to either escape or begin a resistance movement. During the Japanese invasion of Korea, my wife told me that her ancestors hid in the mountains to avoid capture and be shipped off to Japan as slaves. One of Jade's ancestors was a rebel in the Donghak Peasant Revolution (1894), who failed to flee to the mountains and was caught and executed by the Joseon government (ruled 1392-1897). My wife also told me that when the North Koreans invaded South Korea in 1950, both her father and mother's families fled to the mountains and stayed with relatives to keep out of the hands of the North Koreans (since both her parents came from middle class families, they would have been high on the North Koreans' list of people to be eliminated). When the tide of the Korean War turned in favor of the United Nations and South Korean armed forces, her parents were able to return from the mountains.

Most Koreans during the centuries learned what plants were edible in the mountains and using the caves and isolated forests they were able to hide in during times of strife. Korean art and literature prominently feature mountains, and many mentions are made of life in the mountains in Korean historical records. Interestingly enough, one of the most prized items that came from Korea's mountains was ginseng. Considered the best in Asia, Korean ginseng was grown in many places in the mountains. Nowadays, most Korean ginseng is grown in special green houses for the best quality. For centuries, Buddhist monasteries were situated in the mountains to escape the repressive control of the royal Joseon government. Today, many South Koreans build their homes in the mountains due to the limited amount of land available.

[A Mountainous Country; Plate 1]
Some mountains outside the City of Gyeongju

Gyeongbok Palace

Without question, Gyeongbok Palace is the largest and grandest of all the palace complexes in Seoul. Originally, the palace complex was built in 1395, just three years after the Joseon Kingdom was founded. In fact, the Joseon Kingdom would be the longest serving dynasty in Korea's long history. The area chosen for Gyeongbok had to have perfect fung shui, and had to be flanked by a mountain as part of the defense of the complex. Like all palaces that came before it, there was a main outer wall surrounding the whole place, followed by a second wall, and then a main entryway for the king's formal retinue. The most significant building was the main hall where the king sat on his throne and where all of his government cabinet met to discuss affairs of state. Beyond that were separate buildings and annexes where the ladies of the court, the government bureaucrats, and a certain number of servants stayed for the night until summoned by the king the next day. Walls cut off parts of the palace complex according to people's rank in the government system. Only the most chosen people could stay within the palace itself. Lesser government workers had to leave the palace complex for the night. The palace had special side doors where government employees not allowed to stay were let out. The king's guards were posted at all entrances at all times, and people could leave and return with special passes. Ordinary people, unless summoned by the king's government, could dare not go into the palace complex. The whole thing was a closed off area forbidden to ordinary people.

Like Korea, Gyeongbok Palace did not have a happy history. The whole complex was burnt down during the Japanese invasion of Korea (1592-1598). The whole palace complex was not rebuilt until 1867. Barely when it was rebuilt, tragedy again struck. The Japanese imperial forces, who were stationed in Korea at the time, smashed into the palace and murdered Queen Myeongseong. Her husband, King Gojong, the ruler of Korea (reigned from 1864-1907), fled the palace never to return again in 1897. After that, the palace fell into disrepair. When the Japanese took over Korea as a colony in 1910, they further destroyed sections of the palace by wrecking or dismantling sections of the complex. When Japan surrendered after World War II in 1945, only ten percent of what was left of Gyeongbok remained. Its sad story was not quite over. During the Korean War (1950-1953), parts of what remained of Gyeongbok were badly damaged, and the main entrance gate was completely destroyed. Just after the war, Gyeongbok Palace remained untouched until restoration work was begun in 1989. The South Korean government has not only repaired what had been damaged but has begun a long-term program of restoring the palace complex to what it originally was in 1897. This work is ongoing, and it is estimated that 50 percent of Gyeongbok has been restored.

The reconstruction of Gyeongbok Palace has been based on two things. First, part of the reconstruction process has been based on surviving records. Despite all of the wars and devastation Korea has sustained over the centuries, Korea's royal records have been fairly complete and consistent. Second, there are a lot of photographs from the 19th and early 20th centuries which provide incredible detail of what Gyeongbok looked like when the Joseon existed. Interestingly enough, Gyeongbok Palace has received far better care from the current South Korean government than the past Joseon government ever gave it. Because of all the people and their country have endured, the people and their government are trying to preserve as much of their past as is possible.

[Gyeongbok Palace; Plate 2]
The Gwanghamun Gate leading into the Gyeongbok Palace complex

[Gyeongbok Palace; Plate 3]
The main throne room in Gyeongbok Palace

[Gyeongbok Palace; Plate 4]
Gyeonghoeru Pavilion Gyeongbok

Deoksu Palace

Built in the late 14th Century A.D., Deoksu Palace was the only palace complex that largely survived the Japanese invasion of Korea when the Japanese burnt all of the others down. Because of this, Deoksu Palace was the seat of administration until 1612, when the larger newly completed Changdeok Palace was built. The royal Joseon government then moved into Changdeok Palace, and Deoksu Palace was relegated to being little more than a military garrison. It would remain this way until Korean King Gojong literally escaped from Gyeongbok Palace because the Japanese military, who had assassinated his wife, fled to the Russian embassy in the middle of the night. King Gojong would stay in the Deoksu Palace for the rest of his life because it was right next to the Russian embassy which had offered him protection against the Japanese. However, when the Japanese won the Russo-Japanese War (1904-1905), the Russians were forced to pull out of Korea. Instead of Deoksu Palace being a haven for King Gojong, it had in effect become a prison since the Japanese would never let him leave. He died there on January 21, 1919.

Ironically, it was at Deoksu Palace that King Gojong proclaimed in 1897 the establishment of the Empire of Korea in a bid to keep Korea as an independent state. Gojong had then taken the title of emperor, which no Korean king had ever done because all Korean monarchs did not want to upset their relationship with China. In the end, this did not matter as the Japanese forced King Gojong to abdicate in 1907 in favor of his son Sunjong, who ruled Korea until the Japanese annexed it in 1910. Gradually, the Japanese dismantled parts of Deoksu Palace to make it little more than a theme park. By the time the Japanese colonial occupation ended, only one-third of Deoksu Palace buildings remained. Deoksu Palace managed to survive the Korean War, and today the South Korean government is trying to preserve Deoksu Palace. One of the strangest all the buildings on Deoksu Palace's grounds is the former royal administration building called Seokjojeon. What makes this structure so unusual is that it is a completely western architectural imperial residence designed by the British architect G.R. Harding. King Gojong wanted to project Korea as an empire that was modernizing along western lines. Seokjojeon was completed in 1907, but this building would be among the last works constructed in Korea before the Japanese took over the country.

Seokjojeon and the rest of the Deoksu Palace could not be more of a contrast in East versus West. Excluding Seokjojeon, the rest of the complex is made of wood, has no chairs (except for the throne the king sat on), and every beam was beautifully carved with ornate designs as well as beautiful Chinese calligraphy. Seokjojeon was western in every manner. The place has elegant chairs, western-style paintings and gold trim on the walls, marble floors, chandeliers, and pristine white walls and ceilings. It is almost like a miniature Buckingham Palace (it most probably was designed to be that) and was a radical departure from how King Gojong lived a decade before. One thing that the Seoul government revived was the changing of the royal guard at Deoksu Palace. With their colorful clothes and beautifully choreographed procession, I found this event a very fitting act that had been done over the centuries at Korea's royal palaces.

Plate 5 Deoksu Palace
[Deoksu Palace; Plate 5]
The main throne room in Deoksu Palace

[Deoksu Palace; Plate 6]
The Courtyard Deoksu Palace

[Deoksu Palace; Plate 7]
The changing of the guard at Deoksu Palace

[Deoksu Palace; Plate 8]
The western style building Seokjojeon Deoksu Palace

Gyeonghui Palace

This is one of the five palaces that is least talked about. The other four palaces are well known. Many people have and continue to visit Gyeongbok, Changdeok, Changgyeong, and Deoksu palaces. When I visited Gyeonghui Palace, the fifth place, there were no other people except my wife and myself. Maybe this was because the fifth palace was a reconstruction of what the original had been. Built in the 17th Century, the palace complex was not exactly used all that much. It was connected to Deoksu Palace by a bridge that no longer exists. One major problem with the palaces was that they were susceptible to fire, and in the 19th Century many of the buildings at Gyeonghui burnt down. A lot of the fifth palace was never rebuilt at the end of the Joseon. When the Japanese took over Korea, they took all remaining buildings of Gyeonghui Palace and moved them elsewhere.

It would not be until the 1990's that the South Korean government would reconstruct the fifth palace. The government brought back those buildings which had survived Japanese rule, and helped to reconstruct the other parts of the palace. One major problem is the fact that a lot of the land which Gyeonghui Palace once occupied is now taken up by the Seoul Museum of History and other modern buildings. Hence, only 33 percent of the palace complex has been reconstructed. Nevertheless, Gyeonghui Palace is a classic example of middle Joseon architecture. The government spared no expense at reconstructing a monumental work, and for me it was an architectural marvel worth seeing.

Located about five city blocks from where I used to live in the Sodaemun district of Seoul, I was entranced by the red wooden columns, and ornate roofs of the main throne room and the side buildings, the beautifully cut stone platforms that are the foundations of the palace, the magnificent cobblestone flooring, and incredibly decorated wall and door panels of the main building. The work done still fills me with a sense of wonder. As I walked from one part of the palace complex to the next, I could hear my footsteps. Even though the noise of car traffic and the bustle people of Seoul was just outside the palace, because there was only my wife and me it felt more quiet and more peaceful being at Gyeonghui than just about anywhere else in that city. On a personal note, Gyeonghui Palace may not be world famous like the pyramids of Egypt, the Great Wall of China, the Kremlin in Moscow, or Machu Pichu in Peru, but this place was and remains special to me because it is an historic place that is not so well known. To me, the obscure places are more precious than the more famous and well-traveled parts of the world.

[Gyeonghui Palace; Plate 9]
The main throne room at Gyeonghui Palace

[Gyeonghui Palace; Plate 10]
Part of the Gyeonghui Palace

Hangul

This is one of the things that is truly Korean. The Chinese have their beautiful writing, and the Japanese have a phonetic writing system called hiragana. But the Koreans developed their alphabet called *hangul* which is comprised of 24 letters. This alphabet was developed in the reign of King Sejong (1418-1450), and the reason it was developed was for the ordinary people to be able to read government edicts. The Koreans adopted Chinese writing because China was the most advanced civilization at the time, and the Koreans had no other writing system for their language. However, two obvious problems emerged with regards to writing the Korean language in Chinese. First, the Chinese writing system was too complex and cumbersome for most Koreans. Also, the Chinese writing did not mirror the Korean pronunciations or how the Korean spoken language sounded like in written form. Hence, hangul was developed for this purpose, and for helping ordinary people to be able to read and write. But as I learned, it went further than that. It helped make it possible for ordinary people to be able to read anything printed.

I remember when I visited the National Museum of Korea, there was an exhibit of printed Buddhist textbooks printed in both Chinese and in hangul. The textbooks were printed between the 14th Century A.D. and the 17th Century A.D. The Buddhist monasteries, in order to gain more converts, started to issue their textbooks and sacred scrolls in hangul. This made a major difference in drawing in ordinary people, and when Christianity was introduced into Korea, the first Christian missionaries also translated the Bible and other written Christian literature into hangul. Despite hangul being a better method of writing Korean, the Joseon Kingdom largely stuck with the Chinese writing system in all official court records, and Korean scholars still had to learn to read and write in Chinese writing. Everything from official Korean money to all government was in Chinese writing and sometimes in hangul. While the scholars and royal court knew how to read Chinese writing, and while all provincial governors knew how to read Chinese writing, the ordinary people did not. Even when King Gojong founded the Empire of Korea, the royal Korean government still used Chinese writing in all official edicts and documentation.

When the Japanese took control of Korea, they made Japanese the official language. They were doing everything they could for ordinary Koreans to speak, read and write in Japanese. In 1938, the Japanese completely banned hangul in Korea, and any and all Korean language publications were banned in 1941. Also, the Japanese colonial authorities did everything they could to make sure Koreans did not even speak their own language in public. After Japan's defeat in 1945, both North and South Korea brought back the hangul alphabet and it became compulsory in all public and private schools. The Chinese writing for the Korean language continued but began to greatly decline in the 1970's. Currently, the only writing system South Koreans use is hangul, and it has become a source of national pride for Koreans. There is even a Hangul Day in South Korea (October 9th), which celebrates the creation of the Korean alphabet.

[Hangul; Plate 11]
Hangul signs for various businesses in the port City of Incheon

A Yangban Estate

The Joseon Kingdom's social order was in so many ways like a pyramid. There was the royal family at the top, the scholars and elite families afterwards, the farmers and tradesmen next to the bottom, and the slaves at the bottom. The elite families who administered the country were called **yangban**. The yangban were an inherited class who were granted their status and privileges by the king. Just as the king could make them yangban, so he could also take away their status. As such, the yangban enjoyed having large estates, servants and slaves, and control over local as well as provincial administration. They also appreciated and practiced the arts, and it was not unusual for members of a yangban family to also be artists, architects, historical record keepers, and court accountants.

My wife and I, while visiting the port City of Incheon, came across an old yangban estate. Yangban homes dot the country, and some are either deep within urban areas or are in secluded mountain and rural towns. The one we found was not far from city center. The yangban estate was surrounded by a white-washed brick wall in the typical style of the Joseon period. Upon entering a doorway, there is the main hallway and building extensions where a yangban family might eat, sleep and go about daily activities. One important thing is that a typical Korean home has no chairs. Everyone sat on the floor as had been custom for centuries, and families used low tables for furniture. Yangban families had richly decorated dressers made of lacquer with shell inlay. It was common during the Joseon for yangban men to practice Chinese calligraphy. Yangban men also practiced poetry, painting and archery. The yangban house we saw had paintings on the wall as well as a small table with brush pens for calligraphy.

The architectural style of the estate was beautiful yet simple. With its tiled roofs and simple folding doors, the buildings could be heated during the winter months using an under-floor heating system called *ondal*. The floors were heated so that the home remained comfortable even during the worst cold snap. Sometimes the yangban home had two floors, although more often the home was a single floor arrangement with connecting buildings. Although some yangban homes might still be occupied, more often than not as my wife and I discovered they were little more than museums or exhibits of what life was like in pre-modern Korea. The former yangban home we saw was just a dusty relic where over 150 years ago people were born, lived and died within the walls of that place. It is a tribute to a life that no longer exists.

[A Yangban House; Plate 12]
The outer wall of a Yangban home

[A Yangban House; Plate 13]
The front building of a yangban home

[A Yangban House; Plate 14]
Inside a yangban scholar's home

A Farmer's Village House

My wife has an uncle who owns an historic farm village house in the town of Puyo. The house, while maintained by my wife's uncle's family, is nevertheless a national treasure according to the South Korean government. The house, over 250 years old, has not changed since it was first built in the middle 18th Century. It was no small miracle that her uncle's family was able to maintain the house as it originally was. In the 1960's and middle 1970's, former South Korean President Park Chung-hee ordered that all farm houses, regardless of their age, were to have tiled roofs. President Park wanted all of South Korea's houses to look "modern." According to my wife, to disobey Park was a crime. Despite this, my wife's uncle's family defied Park and the roof remained made of thatched straw. This is how Korean farm houses were built originally, and her uncle argued that as an historical house it had to remain the way it was. It was no small miracle that her uncle was able to keep the house as it originally was.

The roof is made from thatched straw, which helps to keep the house cool in the summer and warm in the winter. Every ten years, the straw has to be replaced. The walls are made of clay, and the window frames are made of wood. The folding doors are made of wood and paper, and there is a blessing in Chinese above the front for good luck. In the back of the house are gardens, and thick clay pots, some of them submerged into the ground, which contained the Korean dish called *gimchee*. Gimchee is made of Chinese cabbage, parsley, and garlic marinated in red pepper sauce. This whole thing is then put into the huge earthen pots to ferment. Gimchee is served as a side dish or an ingredient for breakfast, lunch and dinner. It is commonly eaten with rice. The farmer's house I saw was pretty neat and well arranged, but as my wife's uncle explained life was pretty hard for the farmers and peasants who lived in homes like this. First, he said, that as many as two or three generations lived under one roof. Needless to say, this kind of dwelling was fairly crowded. Second, farm families had to work on small plots of land which was not always easy to produce enough food for them. Finally, such life was hard and with the lack of modern medicines most people died early. Few lived to old age.

There were a couple of reasons why my wife's uncle preserved this place as it was. Obviously, her uncle wanted to preserve the past as it was. He wanted to keep his ancestors' home as original as possible. He wanted to show how life was, and how hard it was for the people in the past. And despite the attempt by one dictator to erase part of the past, my wife's uncle has preserved history despite attempts to "modernize" the past. Fortunately, my wife's uncle was far from being the only one who tried to preserve the past. There are hundreds of other such farmer's homes across the country. They have remained as they were when these homes were built hundreds of years ago.

[A Yangban House; Plate 15]
My wife's uncle's ancestral home

[A Farmer's House; Plate 16]
The front entrance to the home

Bulguksa and Cheomseongdae

There is no other Buddhist temple like it on the Korean peninsula. The headquarters of the Jogye Order of Buddhism, what is now Bulguksa was first built in 774 A.D., during the Shilla Kingdom which ruled the whole Korean peninsula from 661 A.D. to 935 A.D. Many palaces and Buddhist temples were constructed during that time period in the present City of Gyeongju, but Bulguksa is one of the few that has relatively survived. The wooden part of the temple was destroyed in the Japanese invasion of Korea, but the stone foundation remained. After the war with Japan, the Joseon Kingdom tried to restore the temple during the next few centuries from the 17th Century A.D. to the 18th Century A.D. However, the Joseon treasury ran out of funds and the temple deteriorated over the next 150 years. Eventually even the stone foundation was falling apart, and by the end of the Joseon Bulguksa was almost a total ruin. It was spared destruction during the Korean War since the North Koreans never got as far as Gyeongju., and renovation work was started on Bulguksa after the war. During the presidency of Park Chung-hee (1961-1979), Bulguksa Temple was completely restored to what it historically looked like in the 8th Century.

As I wandered through the temple complex, I always wondered how much of it is original and how much of it is a reconstruction? A good part of it is a reconstruction. Even if there were no wars and no foreign occupations, nothing lasts forever. Having been to Europe, I realized that few things on that continent were over 1,000 years old. No matter how much effort has been put in to preserve the past, there is a limitation to what has survived. Christian churches in Europe for the most part are less than 1,000 years old, and those that are well over 1,000 years old are only a small percentage of all the churches that exist on the whole continent of Europe today. One thing that is still very much original and still very much intact are the two pagodas at Bulguksa. One is a fairly decorative pagoda called *Dabotap*, and is believed to have been built in 751 A.D. The other, called *Seokgatap*, is believed to have also been constructed in 751 A.D., the same year as Dabotap. Seokgatap, unlike Dabotap, is simple in design, and does not feature any ornate decorations. One thing that Seokgotap did have were holy Buddhist relics found within the structure in 1966. They included a bronze Buddha, a bronze mirror, silk, perfume, and prayer beads. Also found was the oldest printed sacred Buddhist text known. That these two stone pagodas had survived for close to 1,300 years is amazing in of itself.

Another thing that is still very much intact is the stone structure called Cheomseongdae. This was built in the 7th Century A.D. as an observatory, and was used throughout the Shilla period. Whenever I went out of my hotel in Gyeongju, I always went to see this magnificent structure. It is considered the oldest known observatory in Asia, and was used by the royal Shilla court to measure the stars for the changing seasons. Every time I looked at Cheomseongdae, I marvel at how advanced the sciences were in Korea for the time period. I always ask myself what else did the Shilla Kingdom build that was scientifically advanced for the time? A lot of their records were lost, and whatever they created has long been since lost to history. Thankfully, what is left tells us a lot about what Korea did have in ancient times.

[Bulguksa and Cheomseongdae; Plate 17]
The front of Bulguksa

[Bulguksa and Cheomseongdae; Plate 18]
Dabotap

[Bulguksa and Cheomseongdae; Plate 19]
Seokgatap

[Bulguksa and Cheomseongdae; Plate 20]
Cheomseongdae

Hanbok

Hanbok, the traditional women's dress in Korea, is something I did not see too much in everyday life. Yes, the hanbok dress is quite elegant and depending on the material can truly look colorful and beautiful. I found out that the more beautiful the hanbok is, the more expensive the material used to make it would cost. Mt wife explained that a hanbok made of the finest Korean silk could cost anywhere between $3,000 to $4,000. And if gold thread were added it could cost another $1,000. Needless to say, this is a good reason why Korean women do not wear hanbok except for special occasions (I was told by my wife that a hanbok dress made with cotton was nowhere near as elegant). The only time I *ever* saw women wear a hanbok dress was when my mother-in-law wore one attending my wedding. Not just her, but four of her sisters also wore hanbok dresses. They were to put it mildly the most elegant ones I had ever seen.

There are a number of shops selling expensive dresses and especially hanbok dresses. Although it is rare, some Korean women do order hanbok dresses for their own weddings (normally, Korean women prefer western-style wedding dresses in an effort to look "modern"). My own wife wore a western-style wedding dress. Could my wife have worn a hanbok? Theoretically it was possible, but by custom I learned it would not have been acceptable. In Korean tradition, traditional clothes could only be worn if both marrying couples were ethnic Koreans. If, for example, one of the couples was not an ethnic Korean, then the clothes normally were not traditional Korean. Since Jade and I were getting married in a Chinese wedding banquet hall, and since I am a westerner, we both wore western-style clothes for our wedding.

The next question is, if hanbok is rare to find, then where can one see hanbok dresses? As I indicated, at special events, in clothing stores, and on beautiful Korean dolls. Like Japan, there are Korean doll makers who create some of the most beautiful dolls I have ever seen. To make the hanbok dresses, doll makers take the cut pieces of Korean silk that had been thrown away from making original hanbok dresses, and turn them into miniature hanbok dresses for their dolls. But making miniature hanbok dresses for dolls is equally an expensive process, and buying a doll with a silk-made hanbok dress can cost hundreds of U.S. dollars. The cheaper Korean dolls had clothes made of cotton or polyester. My wife explained that the more expensive Korean dolls were bought by Japanese tourists who knew what the quality of those dolls with real silk-made hanbok dresses were. One woman who had a doll shop near Deoksu Palace sold some of the most beautifully made Korean dolls I had ever seen. Yes, she sold these dolls to Japanese tourists (an expensive hotel that catered to Japanese tourists was right above her store, so many Japanese tourists frequented her area), who truly appreciated the quality that went into making these dolls and the hanbok dresses they wore.

[Hanbok; Plate 21]
Expensive dolls wearing hanbok, part 1

[Hanbok; Plate 22]
Expensive dolls wearing hanbok, part 2

[Hanbok; Plate 23]
A Hanbok specialty store

The Christian Impact

The one religion that had a powerful impact on Korea was Christianity. Christianity actually arrived in Korea in the late 18th Century from Koreans who had converted to the Roman Catholic Christian faith during their time in China. Protestant Christianity did not really arrive until the later half of the 19th Century. At first, Christianity was tolerated. However, vicious persecution occurred where thousands of Korean Catholic Christians were massacred in the 1860's. But when King Gojong came to power, he changed the country's policy towards Christianity. Western missionaries came to Korea, and many Koreans of all classes were converted to the new religion. In many ways this was not unusual because so many Koreans were unhappy about the rigid class system under the Joseon Kingdom. For many Koreans, Christianity gave an equal footing with each other.

In many ways, Christianity was important in creating the modern Korean nation and the Korean identity. This is why I saw so many churches and Christian symbols in South Korea. With the exception of the Philippines, South Korea has the largest number of Christians in Far East Asia. An estimated 25 percent of all South Koreans are Christian; it is on an equal par with 25 percent of all South Koreans identifying as Buddhist. Despite attempts by the Japanese colonial government to try and eradicate all of the churches from the peninsula, Korean Christians and Christianity survived and after the end of the Japanese colonial occupation and the Korean War has thrived in South Korea. Korean Christian organizations have sent missionaries all over the world, and have also built homes, hospitals, and hospice care facilities in South Korea and in many other countries. A number of historical churches built during the late Joseon period survive to this day, and many of the early missionaries who came to Korea to convert people to their faith are buried in Seoul and many other cities.

On a personal note, my own wife is a Christian. Her family had converted to Christianity during the Japanese colonial period, and she became an ardent Christian when she was a college student. Like Buddhism, the early Christian missionaries translated their bibles into Korean and used the Hangul alphabet to teach Christianity to the masses. Korean converts did the same thing, and the religion took hold. Today, one can find just about every branch of Christianity from Roman Catholic to most of the Protestant churches to Eastern Orthodox faiths in South Korea. But not just churches are the only sign of Christianity in the country. There is also a holy shrine called Jeoldusan which is in memorial to 6,000 Korean Catholics who were beheaded by the Joseon government in 1866 during one of the persecutions of Christians in the country. It stands as a testament that those who suffered and died will never be forgotten.

Plate 24 First Methodist Church in Seoul

Plate 25 Jeoldusan Martyr's Shrine

Plate 26 Saint Kim Daegun

Ganghwa Island

To get to Ganghwa Island, it was necessary to go by ferry. The trip took about 45 minutes, and Jade and I disembarked on the island's shoreline. From there we caught a bus and traveled through the narrow mountainous roads to Bomunsa Buddhist Temple. We stayed for about a couple of hours before we had some lunch. Jade and I admired the beautiful mountains in the background as we enjoyed a traditional Korean dish known as gimbap. Gimbap looks very much like a Japanese nori roll, but unlike a nori roll which only has fish, a gimbap roll can have beef, vegetables, and egg. Fortunately, Jade and I got to Ganghwa Island early, because we learned that the last ferry left the island in the early evening. After spending half the day on Ganghwa Island, we left for the port city of Incheon.

Technically, Ganghwa Island is part of Incheon. Even though it is separated by water, people from Ganghwa Island regularly go to Incheon and people from Incheon and other parts of South Korea go to Ganghwa Island. Today, access to Ganghwa Island is much easier than it was when we visited there because there are two bridges that connect the island to Incheon. Ganghwa Island has played an important part in Korean history. Koreans have lived on Ganghwa Island for 2,000 years, and the island is dotted with Buddhist temples as well as ancient fortresses that guarded the island from invasion. During the Mongol invasions of the 13th Century A.D. and the Japanese invasion from 1592-1598, Ganghwa Island served as a sanctuary for both the Goryeo (the dynasty that came before the Joseon, and ruled Korea from 935 to 1392 A.D.) and Joseon royal governments. Even though Korea had been conquered by the Mongols, the Goryeo government still functioned as an act of defiance against these invaders. Because Ganghwa Island is so close to North Korea, it is a lookout post against any possible North Korean invasion.

Plate 27 Bomunsa Temple Part 1

Plate 28 Bomunsa Temple Part 2

Cheondogyo

Unlike Buddhism and Christianity, Cheondogyo started in Korea. This religion began as a revolt against the Korean monarchy in 1860 under the leadership of Ch'oe Che-u. Initially called the Donghak Peasant Movement, it led a massive revolt against the Joseon monarchy in 1894. This rebellion was crushed by the Joseon with the help of the Japanese Imperial Army. Nevertheless, the Donghak Peasant Movement continued, and eventually started to evolve into a religion under the leadership of Son Byong-hi that is known today as Cheondogyo.

Cheondogyo encompasses Korean shamanism, and in Cheondogyo belief an individual must cultivate one's self to be in touch with Heaven and the Divine Master of all creation Haneullim. These concepts in Cheondogyo take from the Korean people the ancient spiritual beliefs that had been part of Korean shamanism for thousands of years. In so many ways, Cheondogyo followers believe that the Korean people are the chosen of Heaven, and that all are equal under Heaven. The Japanese colonial authorities tried to suppress Cheondogyo because of its highly nationalistic nature (Cheondogyo activists were heavily involved in the March 1st Independence uprising in 1919, something that greatly spooked the Japanese), but all they succeeded in doing was driving the Cheondogyo religious movement underground until the Japanese lost in World War II. Despite the fact that this is a very modern movement, it is a very real Korean historical phenomenon, and Cheondogyo holds a venerable place in South Korean society. There are 380 Cheondogyo temples throughout South Korea.

I visited the Cheondogyo Central Temple in Seoul a number of times. It is a modern brick building completed in 1923, and it is simple yet elegant. The inside of the temple can hold hundreds of believers during services. Interestingly enough, the Cheondogyo Central Temple had their religious literature printed in both Korean and English. Perhaps the literature was for interested westerners, or people of Korean ancestry visiting the country? I found the temple interesting, and the people there very friendly.

Plate 29 Cheondogyo Central Temple in Seoul

Modern Seoul

I would be amiss if I did not say anything about the city I lived in for one year and had gone back to time and again. Seoul, one of the largest cities on earth, has a history of close to 700 years, and is the headquarters of not only the South Korean government but of the well-known corporations Samsung, Hyundai, KIA, LG, Lotte, and Korean Air (which I always took from the United States to South Korea and back). In so many ways it was and remains an ultra-modern city with among the best Internet connections and telecommunications network in the world. Few cities in the world even close to Seoul, and South Korea has some of the best educated people. Above all else, South Korea prizes those with the best education. Those who attained university degrees from Korea University, Yonsei University, and Seoul National University are considered the best of the best. The South Koreans who were able to get into these institutions make-up many of South Korea's highest business corporate heads, best medical personnel, highest serving court justices, richest citizens, and senior political officials.

It was my honor to have been an English teacher at ELS Korea, and to have served some of the best and brightest South Koreans in the country. My students were employees at Samsung, Hyundai, KIA, LG (then known as Gold Star), Lotte, and Korean Air. My students were also from Korea University, Yonsei University, and Seoul National University. These people became my friends, my contacts with everyday South Korean life, and they helped me learn about their beautiful and magnificent country. One of these students became my most beloved wife. Originally a nurse at Korea University Medical Center, she had worked there for 18 years. She had met famous actors, journalists, comedians, and even one of the future presidents of South Korea Kim Young-sam. She worked on a distinguished team of nurses and doctors who provided the medical care in the country. Whenever I went to Seoul, my wife would show me the best museums, the great historic sites, the five palaces, and take me to places with really good Korean food.

Looking back, I always wonder if some of my students helped to invent the great telecommunication devices now being used such as wifi, the smart phone, and computer tablets that hundreds of millions of people use all over the world? Samsung was instrumental in this technology revolution so many countless people take for granted. It is hard to believe that a small country like South Korea, with such ancient roots and in a remote corner of the world, could have had such a great impact on the world. Nevertheless, it has, and my personal relation with this country, people and culture has touched my life in a way that it will be a major part of who I am. For my wife and me, South Korea will always be a part of our lives.

Plate 30 Modern Seoul

Plate 31 Downtown Chogno Street in Seoul

Plate 32 Some of My Students Part 1

Plate 33 Some of My Students Part 2

Plate 34 Jade and Myself

Printed in the United States
by Baker & Taylor Publisher Services